T0121932

INDIGO SCOUT

come closer, your purpose is calling

ARNETTE LAMOREAUX

BALBOA.
PRESS

A DIVISION OF HAY HOUSE

Author Credits:
The Indigo Soul: a child's journey to purpose

Images provided by:
Erynn Lamoreaux
Natalie Stott
Daniel Viotto

Special thanks to my new and supportive friend, Eileen Poldermans, a gifted artist based in Australia. She has graciously shared her painted images for Animal Affinity Indigo, Meditation and Mikao Usui.

Balboa Press books may be ordered through booksellers or by contacting:

Balboa Press
A Division of Hay House
1663 Liberty Drive
Bloomington, IN 47403
www.balboapress.com
1 (877) 407-4847

Printed in the United States of America.

ISBN: 978-1-4525-2097-1 (sc)
ISBN: 978-1-4525-2099-5 (hc)
ISBN: 978-1-4525-2098-8 (e)

Library of Congress Control Number: 2014915597

Balboa Press rev. date: 10/21/2014

*I lovingly dedicate this book to
wondrous Indigo Scouts.
You entrusted me with who you are,
fulfilling God's Will for us all.*

CONTENTS

FORWARD

By Karen Viotto

GoIndigo™ Director Learning & Development

Indigo Reiki Master Teacher

It is so apparent to all of us who know Arnette well that she was intended to write this book. As her friend and colleague, I can honestly say that I have never seen anyone put this much drive and passion into a project. She has strived and fought for her own Indigo children, diligently ensuring they are happy, confident, and balanced, which is not an easy task in a society where they are left to feel anything but "normal." However, her fight has not ceased with her own children. Arnette is determined to reach all Indigo Souls, not only through her books, but through many other avenues. Learning Centers are being developed where the gifts of an Indigo will be "unlocked." Processes are in place that will help guide the Indigo, with open arms, to their divine purpose. Those who choose this path will be honored and supported as they begin to pursue a life as the gifted healers they are meant to be. Indigo will help heal, people, animals, and even the Earth. This is an extraordinary undertaking, the first of its kind, focused solely on the Indigo Souls and their ability to be great healers.

Many years ago I would have thought this was all too kooky. But I have witnessed and experienced too much for me to ignore or claim that the experiences that have led Arnette and me to this day are just due to someone's colorful imagination. The compelling events that have unfolded are too numerous to even count. I truly believe that this book is the beginning of something big, something that will promote a shift in a positive direction and one that is so desperately needed at this time in our history.

What is my role in all this? I am a teacher. I have been one my entire adult life. I have studied and taught the natural sciences in many different capacities to all age groups. I have known many Indigo Souls, long before I was even aware of the concept.

Indigo Soul, you were that 13 year old boy in my class with a certain light in your eyes, that is, until you were made to be comatose by the drug Ritalin. This broke my heart. It wasn't your parents' fault. They didn't know any better. They may have been pressured. I didn't understand why other teachers found you to be a problem. Maybe you were fed up with sitting still for hours at a time being forced to silently fill out work sheets. It was clear to me what the "problem" was. "Put him in my class", I said. Together, we discovered the microbe world under the microscope. We learned about metamorphosis, not from a worksheet, but by caring for and observing mealworms as they gradually changed into winged beetles. You were so excited to learn! Like an archaeologist, you skillfully extracted a rodent skull from an owl pellet. Much to the horror of some teachers, you wore the skull around your neck with the string I provided you! It was Halloween after all!

Like those funny mealworms, I too have morphed over the years. My life has lead me to this day, a day where my visions are rich with scenes of those who are Indigo doing extraordinary things in a place where their natural gifts provide healing. I write this with tremendous gratitude for all that Arnette is bringing forth, and for all that is Indigo.

PREFACE

My own spiritual path unfolded as I tried to understand how, and for what reason, my children were different. I learned I have the Archetype of Navigator. A Navigator is the parent or guardian of an Indigo Soul. As a Navigator it is my responsibility to guide, guard, and protect the soul(s) in my care. If you believe that your child is Indigo, there is a different message to help you find the way. Please reach for the book titled *The Indigo Soul: a child's journey to purpose*, the first collaboration between Abraham and me.

For this installment of messages, the intended audience is an Indigo Soul who is older, wiser, yet still seeking his or her truth (also referred to as an Indigo Scout). I am blessed with the ability to hear Abraham in regard to the Indigo Soul. From that blessing, it is my privilege to write and teach on behalf of Abraham, so that we may all learn to love, honor and respect the souls that are Indigo. It is important for all humanity to understand why they are here.

~Arnette

LAYING THE FOUNDATION

The year is 1999. I'm 35 years old. My son is five and my daughter is one. There is a book on the market making quite a sensation (and considered quite controversial) called "The Indigo Children" by Lee Carroll and Jan Tober. I'm stating this fact because the term "Indigo" isn't anything new. The term, along with many books on the subject, has been around for quite some time. Let's give credit where credit is due. This book brought awareness to the fact the Indigo are here.

Fast forward 10 years when I learn my own children are Indigo. Of course I went in search of a book. I'd look at the pretty cover, read the back, and purchase it. Some I barely started, most I never finished, except one: "The Care and Feeding of Indigo Children" by Doreen Virtue (Hay House, May 2001). It resonated with me. I read that book from front to back in the parking lot. Only once, I never read it again. I did purchase extra copies to hand out if the situation warranted it. I still recommend it to this day. Yet I must have subconsciously known that I didn't require anyone else's opinion. From that day forward, I did not read any other books about Indigo.

My only source, for and about Indigo, is Abraham.

It wasn't obvious to me then, but it is obvious to me now. If I was to really "hear" what Abraham was going to share with me, I could not be inadvertently influenced by something I might have read years before. I am not in the medical profession. I'm just a mom doing the best I can with something that is totally out of my "normal." "What" is Indigo or "who" is Indigo was relevant, but it is not what fueled me. So what if my children are Indigo. What exactly does that mean? What am I supposed to do with that? I wanted to know WHY. *Why Indigo?*

If you are not yet familiar with Abraham: Abraham is a group consciousness of highly evolved spiritual beings; beings that work through God. Their purpose is to bring humanity the wisdom and guidance of God for the advancement of our soul's journey. Though most of their work is done through human channels, Abraham does not function with ego (a human characteristic). They have chosen multiple people to work through in delivering their messages. The most well known channel is Esther Hicks. She has been channeling messages and writing books with them for over 30 years.

Abraham also works with my own mentor Linda Drake[1]. It was through Linda that I was first introduced to Abraham. I was soon gifted, just as Esther and Linda were gifted, to receive messages from Abraham.

~Arnette

---

[1] **Linda Drake** – Life path Healer/Intuitive Life Coach – http://lindadrakeconsulting.com

ABRAHAM MAKES CONTACT

I spent a lot of time, energy and money searching for an answer as to why my children struggle with traditional education. I have pushed every imaginable boundary of the one belief I did have and held tight to, a belief in *logic*. Everything you read will seem "far out there", and it is. Yet it is also my truth and this gives me me courage to share it.

In the fall of 2012, I received a call from Linda Drake, my life path healer/intuitive life coach. It's out of the ordinary for Linda to call me. "Hello?" I answered. "Hello Arnette. This is Linda Drake." She cut right to the chase, "I have a woman in session right now, and your name came up. Apparently you know something or someone that can help her with her business, do you mind giving her a call?" "Um, sure, okay," I said. I let two days pass and I called and left a message something like, "Hi, my name is Arnette, Linda Drake asked me to call indicating that I might be able to help you with a work issue, thanks (feeling just a tad bit awkward) bye." We played phone tag but we eventually connected. She was the owner of a local business looking to hire her #2 person, and literally, within two minutes the name "Dan Viotto" popped into my head. Clear as day. I interrupted her and said, "I think I know your person, I don't even know if he's looking for a job, but I'll ask him." There was excitement in her voice. "You know my person?" she asked. "Yes....yes, I think I do."

Long story short, she and my friend Dan did connect and he did end up working at her company for awhile. There you have it Arnette; I say to myself, tangible proof for your logical little brain that you "hear." It's been a fun story to tell, but it gets so much better.

Four months later, I feel like I need to see Linda again. It has been awhile and it helps me have these touch points with Abraham (through her), along with my own Spirit Guides and Angels. Over the years, I've read many wonderful books authored by Esther and Jerry Hicks. As with Esther and Jerry, Linda has been blessed to work with Abraham too. I cover the same discussion points every time: my son, my daughter (both Indigos), my parents, my work, myself. I remind myself to schedule an appointment; it may take some time for an opening. In addition, I think I need to participate in Reiki III training so I have a better understanding of what Jacob (my son) will be able to do. I can't just sign up. I need to be invited to participate. I think that might be pushing my skill set just a little bit.

Since I have an hour before I need to pick up my daughter. I can either a) do some work, or b) meditate. It's been a long time since I've really meditated. No one is home, no distractions. I settle in for what hopes to be a good session, maybe I'll see my teacher Spirit Guide (Chief) who is always beautiful red. Maybe I'll see black and white photographs flip through so fast I have to ask them to slow down. I always hope I experience something versus falling asleep.

My head is *hurting*. I think this is what a migraine feels like though I've never had a migraine so I'm not sure. Like "stick a knife into my skull" kind of hurt. I see the most amazing metallic shimmering gold. And then I hear "it" clear as day, just like I did before. It's not a sound; it's not even really a voice. It's just the words "We gave you Dan Viotto." (Referring to my friend Dan whose name had come up in a session and resulted in a job offer). Startled? Definitely!

My response, "Who's we?" "**We are Abraham**". Holy smokes! What is happening? I can feel one tear slide down my right cheek. I was very aware of that one tear. I had so many questions, but I was so scattered. This is some of what I can remember:

Arnette: You gave me Dan Viotto because I needed tangible proof that what I was "hearing" was real.

Abraham: Of course.

Arnette: Jake (my son) really needed a car. Did we do the right thing in getting him a new car?

Abraham: Jacob requires reliable transportation to do his work.

Arnette: I'm very interested in past life regression; I think that is something I would like to explore.

Abraham: Interesting, but not necessary.

Arnette: I would really like to see auras; I think that would be really cool.

Abraham: That is not your purpose.

Arnette: What is my purpose?

Abraham: To teach what you have learned. To speak the words of Abraham regarding Indigo Souls.

Arnette: Indigo Children?

Abraham: No Arnette, Indigo Souls.

Arnette: I need to meet with Linda.

Abraham: Linda Drake will discuss with you how to write with us.

Arnette: Thank you Abraham.

Abraham: You are most welcome Arnette.

Abraham: Arnette, we shall speak again on Saturday.

I awoke from meditation dumbfounded. Looking in the bathroom mirror there was not the trace of just a single tear; my entire face was wet with tears. I called the next day and left a message to schedule an appointment. I received a call from Linda directly. They've had a cancellation, can I come tomorrow? Abraham can make things happen.

So many people have a wonderful mentor/ teacher in Linda. Jacob and I, along with my friend Karen Viotto, were all invited for Reiki III instruction. How blessed are we! I assumed it was because I will be assisting Jake with his development, but Linda says no. It is because I need to raise my own vibration to work and write with Abraham. I was very excited about this amazing opportunity. I was also apprehensive. This is totally out of my comfort zone. I do not feel worthy. Nor do I think I'm qualified to be working with Abraham. Who am I? I'm just a mom with two Indigo kids.

~Arnette

WHY ARNETTE

We have chosen you, Arnette, to hear our word and to be our voice to benefit humanity. You volunteered for this long ago, knowing that it would require tenacity and an overwhelming sense of right and wrong. Yet, right and wrong is not always black and white. "Right" is what is best for a soul. "Wrong" is what is harmful to a soul. If the rules and regulations of mankind do not have the best interest of the soul, then it is your job, as the guardian of this soul, to determine "its" right and wrong, which is, and will always be, very different from the right and wrong of mankind as you know it. You have been blessed by Source as you understand through actual experiences what it means to be the guardian of an Indigo.

This is a covenant, between Arnette Lillen Lamoreaux, and we that are Abraham, to bring forth the voice of Source. To guide, guard, and protect the soul of the Indigo to navigate paths, journey together, and find purpose here on Earth. You, Arnette, will lovingly guide these souls we bring you. To embrace the uniqueness that is theirs and theirs alone so they may bring forth the healing that is so desperately needed at this time.

We that are Abraham are a collective being that work through Earth Angels, one of which is Arnette Lamoreaux. We lovingly embrace the uniqueness of each and every soul sent to Earth. If you are an Indigo Scout who is feeling lost at sea, look no further. You have found the lighthouse. She will guide you to shore.

~ Abraham

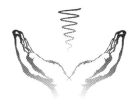

QUESTIONS & ANSWERS

ARE THE CURRENT PERCEPTIONS AROUND INDIGO WRONG?

The current belief in and around Indigo is not wrong, but there is so much MORE. Indigo children have been described as "...bright, intuitive, strong-willed, sometimes self-destructive individuals. They are often labeled - and misdiagnosed - as having ADD or ADHD because they won't comply with established rules and patterns. They also may exhibit behavioral problems at home or in school."[2] Additional books and websites on the subject of Indigo provide lists of characteristics that are valid when describing commonalities amongst Indigo behavior. The same is true when talking about adults.

I personally do not view Indigo as a "label" with negative connotations associated to it. I use the term Indigo to "identify"

---

2   Doreen Virtue, The Care and Feeding of Indigo Children (Hay House, Inc. 2001).

something, just as I would cheese. If I have two types of cheese that look the same, how do I know if one is provolone and the other is mozzarella? I need a label or an identifier. I'm non-Indigo. My children are Indigo. My son does not have ADD or ADHD, however, my daughter is Dyslexic. Though ADD/ADHD may be a common characteristic of Indigos, a child is not Indigo because he/she is ADD/ADHD. However, realizing a child is Indigo is critical as to how they should be nurtured and educated. So yes, please, give them a label.

~Arnette

There are many wonderful resources available that discuss the topic of Indigo Children and Indigo Adults. We must clarify that Indigo refers to a **soul**. The soul does not ever stop being Indigo. Souls come to Earth through conception and birth so naturally they begin their journey as infants and grow to adulthood. To be "Indigo" does not *go away*. A person does not grow into it or out of it. **Simply put, Indigo refers to a person who has a higher vibrational energy, and so has the natural ability to provide healing above and beyond the ability of a non-Indigo person.** *How* that healing transpires is discussed later.

Indigo is not a medical diagnosis, it is a spiritual diagnosis.

**Indigo is not a way to explain or justify behavior.
Indigo is a *purpose*.**

~Abraham

WHY ARE THE INDIGO HERE?

The Indigo Soul is meant to heal
through Source energy.

Disease, any disease, can be healed through Source Energy. Indigo Souls are meant to transmit Source. Actually, any person can be schooled in the art of healing (to transmit Source). However, an Indigo, though you look the same on the inside, you are not the same. An Indigo's energy, surrounding you, living in you, it is you, can transmit a higher energy wave pattern for a longer period of time. It is really quite simple. What mankind has been missing is the conduit that is specially made for the energy that you seek.

The Indigo is a specially made
conduit for Source energy.

Think of electricity flowing through a wire. If too much electricity is surged through a wire that was not meant to hold that amount, the wire may short circuit. Yet, if the wire was intended to allow an unlimited quantity of electrical current, the energy will continue to flow with little to no resistance. Any soul can be educated to flow Source Energy (think of healing with white light). However, an Indigo Soul's purpose is to radiate Source Energy. Indigo refers to the essence of your energy. And yes, it is Indigo blue light.

Indigo must begin to heal that which is broken: the planet, the animals, but most of all, each other. They are here to bring balance back to Earth. Indigos are meant to blend their energy, alongside source (God's) energy, to make it safe for the next wave of souls that are coming.

**To be the receiver of Source Energy
through an Indigo Soul,
is truly a gift from God.**

~Abraham

WHO IS INDIGO?

There is a vast population of Indigo Souls on planet Earth. There are also many individuals who claim to be Indigo when in actuality they are not. A parent may say their child is Indigo because they try to excuse why their child might be considered different. Ego is a characteristic of humanity, yet it is not a characteristic of Indigo. Assumptions are based on collected data, characteristics and behavioral comparisons. Based on Yes or No checkmarks, the descriptor of "Indigo" might be applied. Some writings emphasize behavioral challenges such as ADD, ADHD, Dyslexia, and others as meaning or "being" Indigo. These characteristics are not automatic precursors of Indigo. They are real and identifiable attributes of personalities which may or may not be associated to an Indigo Soul.

It is not to say that one human life is less than, or more than, another human life. It is simply a way to identify an individual who will grow up to be, or who already is, a naturally gifted healer. The world is filled with non-Indigos that are very enlightened, spiritual, beings a well.

~Abraham

COULD YOU BE INDIGO?

Is taking an assessment test a way to identify Indigo? Not recommended, as the result is still only an assumption. By taking a blood test? Certainly not.

An Indigo Soul already "knows" they are Indigo. To provide clarification or understanding they may research and ultimately come to that conclusion, but not because they are told, as a child might be told. They know because they "feel within their being" a *shift* when the word is presented to them. Indigo knows Indigo. It is very apparent when Indigos interact as they sense familiarity, peacefulness, awareness. However a perfectly acceptable way is to just *ask*.

~Abraham

ASK WHOM?

If you are reading this it is because you suspect, or you may even already have validation, that you are Indigo. There are many Earth Angels that can ask on your behalf. However, there are unfortunately people that would tell you yes, even though the answer is actually no. As we know the answer will be true; seek out the GoIndigo™[3] team. The GoIndigo™ team will be able to help you understand if you are indeed Indigo. We are who brought them together. This is their truth. You either are Indigo or you are not. There is no ego involved in asking or in the telling Indigo cannot be learned. It cannot be forced. You either are or you are not.

~Abraham

HOW DOES GOINDIGO™ ASK?

With your permission, or the permission of a parent or guardian if the soul is young, an individual that is trained can ask <u>your</u> "highest self" on <u>your</u> behalf. An individual that is clairaudient (someone that can hear outside the range of normal perception) can "hear" the answer. The use of a pendulum[4] will provide more "tangible" proof and it is most fun to watch.

~Abraham

---

[3]   GoIndigo™ is a non-profit organization dedicated to the ongoing learning and development of Indigo Souls.

[4]   Pendulum - A tool commonly used by healers in order to receive a yes or no confirmation (gauged by energy) to a question that was posed.

Individuals that are raised in Western Culture, more so than anywhere else on Earth, may find themselves uncomfortable with a holistic answer. If your own beliefs are being tested, meaning there is much more in this universe than just you... have faith. Maybe this is why you are reading our message.

~Abraham

WHAT IS MEANT BY INDIGO SCOUT?

The planet has been moving toward crisis for years. God previously sent Indigo *Scouts*. The intent was for these souls to find their purpose with little to no guidance; after all they had been here before! With parents and guardians that were unprepared to understand anything about their child, left to their own devices, most of these souls unfortunately conformed to society and were unable to find their way. Some did create a path that was a hybrid of a traditional career with their true purpose as a healer, some, but not enough.

Are you past the age of needing the permission of a parent or guardian? Do you have free will to do what you want, go where you want, when you want? As you read this, you may feel energy building in you, through you. As Indigo, the energy *is you*.

Maybe you already have found a path as a healer, maybe not. Maybe you are already fulfilled with the life choices you have made for yourself, maybe not. Maybe you are passionate about the contributions you are making to society, maybe not. Only you can determine if you feel a part of you remains unfulfilled. Listen closely Indigo Scout, is your purpose calling?

~Abraham

WHAT ABOUT NON-INDIGO HEALERS?

Earth has been blessed with many Earth Angels and Light Workers that have worked diligently to break down the barriers to holistic healing. They have done a tremendous job at keeping many types of practices alive and available to those who seek them out. Are the Indigos meant to replace those that have dedicated their lives to healing? No! The world can never have enough healers. Their skills will always be very much needed. However, it is imperative that we assist the Indigos in learning their craft quickly and effectively. There is no time to waste!

~Arnette

Earth is meant to have both populations: Indigo and non-Indigo, living in harmony. Helping each other have a wonderful, beautiful, fulfilling human existence. All holistic healers should be honored and respected. Many healers have spent their entire adult life honing a skill that must be passed on so as not to be lost. Share your knowledge with the Indigo Souls. After all, it is the Indigo Souls whom God sent specifically to bring balance back to Earth.

~Abraham

PREPARE YOUR BODY...

OWN YOUR WELLNESS

Walk, outside. Nature is good for your soul. Find a walking trail versus a sidewalk or road. **Hiking** is another excellent preferred activity. Any activity that is engaging Mother Earth will provide both mental and physical rewards.

Swim, outside. Not in a pool of hardened concrete and chemicals. Find a stream, lake, or ocean, as water is soothing to the body, which brings relaxation to the mind, and peace to the soul.

Introduce **meditation** into your routine. Meditation is to intentionally put forth effort to train the mind into a relaxed state of consciousness. Some people prefer guided meditation, where a teacher walks you through steps of visualization. Others prefer listening to soft music or the sounds of nature. Begin with 5 to 15 minutes a day. Gradually work up to no time constraints and find that meditation can last for as long as it is meant!

Begin with whatever **Yoga** you feel comfortable with. It will assist in all aspects of being Indigo. Eventually, it is important to transition into practicing **Kundalini Yoga.** Kundalini Yoga focuses on breath and movement. It is one of the more spiritual types of yoga which goes beyond the physical performance of poses. The energy that lies dormant at the base of the spine until activated is channeled upward through the chakras. Kundalini will help the Indigo harness their energy, allowing it to flow seamlessly and with fluidity, *within* God's Source Energy.

The synergy[5] of Indigo energy is very, very powerful. Especially when purposely coordinated.

Your initial reaction may be, "That is unacceptable; I do not have that kind of time." Finding time is a choice. Preparing your wellness is a must.

~Abraham

---

[5]   Ray French, Charlotte Rayner, Gary Rees, Sally Rumbles, "Synergy is the creation of a whole that is greater than the sum of its parts", Organizational Behaviour (2008).

From the Inside Out

The internal working of your body is more than likely a science experiment gone wrong. The amount of chemicals and toxins you have ingested over the years, intentionally or unintentionally, will negatively impact your ability to reach your highest vibrational point. Not only is it important for you take care of your emotional well-being, it is also important that you detoxify your physical body and introduce healthier habits to maintain an overall energy balance.

Clay

Everyone on planet Earth would benefit from clay detoxification.

Ingest Calcium Bentonite Clay[6]. Once in the digestive track, the clay immediately begins to bind with toxins. Not only environmental toxins, but also with those that occur naturally as by-products of the body's own health processes, such as metabolic toxins. The body has no problem ridding itself of the clay. The clay assists the body's natural eliminatory process by acting as a bulking agent, (similar to fiber) ridding itself of leftover material that doesn't need to be there. Clay is not digested in the same manner as food. Instead, it stimulates the

---

[6] The information herein is meant to supplement and not to be a substitute for professional medical care or treatment. This information should not be used to treat a serious ailment without prior consultation with a qualified health-care professional.

muscles where contractions normally occur to move food and stool through the bowels. The clay, with the adsorbed toxins, is eliminated. Not one part of the body is left untouched by the clay's healing properties.

Once metal levels have been reduced, not only will the physical body of an Indigo benefit from the inside out, their vibration will encounter less interference as it radiates Source Energy.

I have gifted The Living Clay[7] product along with 2 glass bottles (with plastic caps) to many Indigo Souls. I believe in the brand and the concept of metal detoxification that much. I myself consume 2 oz. every morning and every night. As an additional benefit, it has helped control my adult acne!

Organic Juicing

Unleash the natural healing power of your body by flooding it with concentrated nutrients and antioxidants. Unleash the natural healing power of your body by ridding

---

built-up toxins. This is the first step toward a long-lasting lifestyle change. Why? It is important for the Indigo Soul to allow its energy to vibrate at its highest potential. As the clay detox pulls the metals out of one's body, organic juice infuses it with the essential minerals not normally reached through standard eating habits. The lifestyle here in Austin encourages living "cleanly." Personally, I have not been a very healthy eater. I barely use my kitchen, let alone know my way around fresh produce. Recently, I was introduced to the concept of raw juicing. I was impressed with my Indigo son who embraced organic juicing so quickly and gained enough confidence to create his own recipes. For a boy that prefers fast food and over processed concoctions, drinking one or two glasses of juice a day is way more than I could have hoped for.

~Arnette

PREPARE YOUR MIND...

RECLAIM YOURSELF

Every soul enters this world *knowing*, 100%, its true purpose for the lifetime it is about to experience. Indigo is a gifted, sensitive being, with the ability of perception of what is not normally perceptible.

At birth, the human body, which encompasses the soul, is immediately dependent, and as such, the soul is influenced by the behaviors and beliefs of others. The joy of life is the ability to choose, to flex the muscle of free will. However, true bliss is fulfilling God's purpose specifically of YOU. It is difficult to stay on the course in remembering purpose when others are blocking your path. The evolution of mankind has introduced many human ideals. Everyone participates in a different way, learning different skills and techniques to achieve desired results. More often than not, instead of embracing the abilities that God gave each of you, they are not nurtured at all, and in some cases even feared. As time passes, the raising of a human being no longer encourages the gift, but rather it suppresses the gift, the soul's gift of knowing.

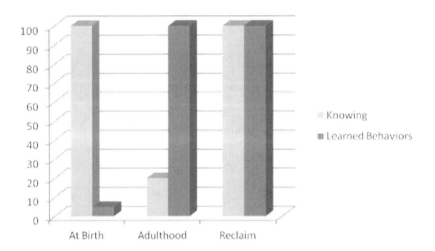

To reclaim your *knowing* is to trust and believe in yourself. More than likely you were raised by parents that attempted to mold you through the same experiences as they themselves were raised. The challenge is that the Indigo Soul was never meant to "be" what this world considered "typical." These souls were never meant to be lawyers, accountants, or mechanics.

Your parents may have been ill-prepared to raise an Indigo Soul, as they tried and tried again to make you something that you are not....like them.

They did the best they could with the knowledge they had at that time. Now it's up to you.

**Take a deep breath, return to basics,
and reclaim your knowing.**

~Abraham

MOVING THROUGH KARMA[8]

A challenge for all people, but especially for an Indigo Scout, is "undoing" perceived restrictions placed on you since you came into this world. Including what may have been brought with you from previous lifetime(s). It is beneficial to assess what may be holding you back both physically and emotionally. Do you have fears, phobias or mental blocks? Do you repeat the same behavior even when it is unhealthy? Every event brings a lesson. You either learn from it or you don't. When you have dissolved or disarmed Karma, you break through your Karmic Veil and step through to Dharma[9].

---

[8]   (formal) Karma: the force created by a person's actions that is believed in Hinduism and Buddhism to determine what that person's next life will be like. (informal) Karma: the force created by a person's actions that some people believe causes good or bad things to happen to that person, Merriam-Webster Dictionary http://www.learnersdictionary.com/definition/karma

[9]   Dharma: Hinduism & Buddhism term, a: the basic principles of cosmic or individual existence: divine law. b : conformity to one's duty and nature, Merriam-Webster Dictionary http://www.merriam-webster.com/dictionary/dharma

It seems the older we are the harder it may be to let go. Be patient. Old habits and thought processes are hard to break.

Growing up with Blame

Do you ever say to yourself "My parents did not understand me. My parents could not relate. My siblings made fun of my emotional sensitivity. My teachers were frustrated with my inability to learn what they were teaching. Other children thought I was too weird and did not want to be my friend." Does any of this sound familiar? Are there more statements that you can add?

It's okay.

There is always a Divine Order to everything. Nothing could have happened sooner, or later, nor should it. It is not too late, it is perfect timing. There is no need to blame anyone, for anything. You are exactly where you are supposed to be, right here, right now.

Growing up with Shame

Do you ever say to yourself "I feel bad that I'm not like everyone else. I had difficulty grasping the social structures in place. I wish I was "more" for my parents. I felt very alone. I didn't feel supported. I felt stupid. I never felt like I belonged...

anywhere." Does any of this sound familiar? Are there more statements that you can add?

It's okay.

There is always a Divine Order to everything. You are not less than, nor are you more than, you are perfect. There is no need to feel shame, for anything. You are exactly who you are supposed to be, right here, right now.

Tapping Therapy

The negative emotions or beliefs that are rooted from past problems or pains, such as blame and shame, can be released leaving you feeling calm and peaceful. Emotional Tapping is a self administered technique similar to acupuncture, but without needles! Using your own finger tips, on specific body points in a particular order, you can learn to balance your energy system. The process is quick, gentle, and easy.

Traditional therapy was not effective for my Indigo son. However, he has benefited tremendously from using an emotional tapping technique called the Thought Field Therapy (TFT) approach founded by Roger Callahan (www.rogercallahan.com). Another source is the Emotional Freedom Technique (EFT) by Gary Craig, who studied under Roger Callahan (www.emofree.com).

AM I READY TO BE A HEALER NOW?

Knowing your natural physical capacity to heal is a wondrous feeling. The *vibration of your being* is already stronger. Awareness of your true purpose may even bring a sense of relief. You can definitely pursue many traditional modalities with success. Massage Therapy, Acupuncture, Yoga, Nutrition, Physical Therapy, the list goes on and on. One of the challenges found with Indigo Souls is the formality of traditional education spanning from the lower grades all the way into University. The approach to learning most institutions adhere to is not conducive to the way an Indigo learns. It definitely is not due to lack of aptitude. Indigo Souls are incredibly intelligent. Though some Indigo Scouts may find these traditional avenues easy to navigate, most do not.

There are other things to consider besides a "skill" to be administered. If the purpose of an Indigo is to be a conduit for Source Energy, you need to increase your vibration. The higher your vibration, the more effective conduit you will be.

This allows for more energy to pass through. It is not only your physical body that must be in top form. It is also your *allowing* of the non-physical world to play a pivotal role in your life. Keep reading!

~Arnette & Abraham

REDEFINE YOUR NORMAL

What is "normal?" As a noun, it means the usual, average, or typical state or condition (Dictionary.com). As an adjective, it means conforming to standard; usual, typical or expected (Dictionary.com). Who came up with those definitions? Who determined that *scale of normalcy*? Why are we scared if our behavior or choices are not status-quo? Why is everyone expected to conform to the same standard of *being normal*?

We challenge the Indigo population to define their own normal. Instead of trying to live within the box society wants to put (and keep) you in, expand the box above and beyond the parameters this normal society has come to expect (of themselves and everyone else). Most importantly, be proud of being Indigo.

~Arnette & Abraham

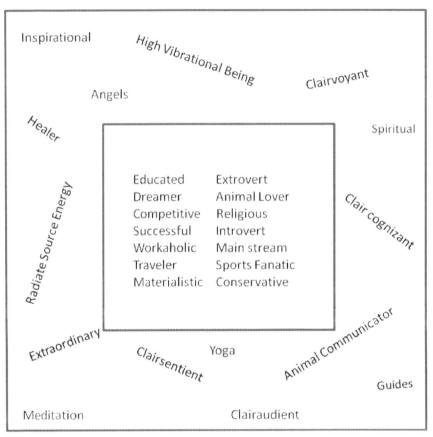

Redefine Your Normal: what's in your box?

PREPARE YOUR SOUL...

GET REAQUAINTED WITH YOUR TEAM

Being part of a team is an amazing synergy. Unfortunately, most people do not utilize the most powerful team available, that of their own Angels and Spirit Guides. Each and every human soul was accompanied to Earth with Angels provided by God (for you and you alone). **Angels** from God have never experienced a human existence; they are as fascinated by you as you are of them. Angels live with you, through you, *for you*. However, God provided very specific guidelines in that an Angel can in no way influence your free will, the ability to have choice, unless asked, by you. They cannot intercede.

Think of it like a sporting event where your family, friends, and Angels are all sitting in the bleachers cheering you on to victory. You fall, and for whatever reason, you cannot get back up. They all sit paralyzed in the stands watching. They so want to come down to join you, to help you, in any way that they can. Your Angels sit there as well, encouraging you to *ask; simply ask*. One simple thought, "please help me," provides them the permission to swoop in and surround you with love, support, and energy. But Angels are not to be called upon when only misfortune happens, quite the opposite! Invite your Angels everywhere! Ask them to surround you in white light to keep you safe on a journey, or to help you know what you need to know, when you need to know it. Bask in their glory and allow them to fulfill *their* true purpose, to walk along side you, as part of you, and experience this life, together.

You may also be blessed with a family member or friend that has left this lifetime and returned home to Source. They too may provide guidance in a time of need and are lovingly referred to as Guardian Angels.

There are Earth Angels[10] that are gifted in communication with Angels. Interestingly enough, Angels like to give you tangible proof of their existence: loose feathers, found coins, or light bulbs constantly going out in your presence. Allow yourself to acknowledge them; it will benefit you both.

Spirit Guides are also part of your team. Unlike Angels, they have had human lifetimes, many human lifetimes, and seek to help you find enlightenment. Everyone has at least four guides. Experience happiness with your **Joy Guide**. Feel safe and secure with your **Protector**. Know you are cared for by

---

[10]   Earth Angel - A Non-Indigo individual who pursued reclaiming their knowing and are gifted working with the non-physical.

your **Alchemist**. And aspire for personal growth through your **Teacher**.

Unfortunately, many societies do not openly welcome discussions about what cannot be seen nor heard. We have asked Arnette to share her experience specific to this topic in the hope that you too will be open and allow your own Spirit Guides to reveal themselves to you.

~Abraham

I'm fortunate here in Austin to have access to gifted Earth Angels that have provided such amazing experiences to me. A local woman, who I found through mutual friends, is blessed with the ability to communicate with Spirit Guides and will provide an introduction. "Sometimes", she explained, "it's easier to have a conversation and reach out for help with someone who has a face and a name."

I was so pleased to have met my Joy Guide "Prissy", whom wondered why we stopped painting, as I found such peace and happiness at my kitchen table. I am talented. My art is matted, framed, and hangs in my home. Prissy said, "You stopped Arnette because you believe every piece has to be perfect, every piece needs to be displayed. You put so much pressure on yourself that you lost the joy." And she was right. Prissy also enjoys roller coasters as well, which really works to my advantage!

Leopold is an extremely large Viking with a long red beard, massive arms and a fairly large belly. He is strong as an ox and as gentle as a bunny. He pokes fun at how uptight I am, and is always trying to encourage me to relax. No harm will come to me; he always has my back, so he says while taking a bite out of a turkey leg. I know he is with me. I found myself in a situation where I could not move to protect myself because acupuncture tends to keep you immobile in that way. I was scared by some strange anomalies that were around me including unexplainable noises. I asked him, "Please make it stop Leopold, whatever is happening is really freaking me out." He did make it stop. I have a witness.

I must admit I do not call on Dr. Frank Barnhardt, my Alchemist, as frequently as I should, especially when I'm feeling under the weather. Even I forget what is available to me in my own tool chest of resources.

When it was time for me to meet my Teacher, he refused to partake. He refused to be introduced. He said, "We have met before, I am insulted she does not recall. She must remember on her own if she is to learn anything." I was embarrassed in front of this woman who was facilitating this session with my guides. I was also very hurt. I was trying to learn, I was trying to grow. I was filled with self-doubt that after all this I'm not good enough to meet my own Teacher!

That night I sat with my pendulum and attempted to relax my mind and allow myself to remember. I asked for guidance to take me back to that point in time where I had met my Teacher. And by God, I did.

I had a dream a few years ago. My dreams are like movies in living color. I was with my parents in the middle of a desert in a circular enclosure. It was surrounded by caves stacked two stories high. Each cave had a very beautiful wooden door with ornate carvings arched around it. Many people were milling around...waiting. But I didn't know what we were waiting for. I glanced up to a second story cave with a window and I could see the flicker of a light, like the room was dark, but a television was on. I saw the shadow of someone walking around. Suddenly, the crowd stilled and then hushed tones said, "He's coming, he is finally coming." The crowd parted to allow this amazing Being to walk through. He was wearing the most vibrant red feathered headdress and wore a long red robe with gold trimming. He was so tall and broad chested. He was regal. He was important. He was walking right toward me. I quickly looked at my parents, yet I was frozen in place. I didn't know what he wanted from me. The word "Shaman" was what I heard. He gently put his hand on my head and smoothed it down gathering my long hair and pulling it over one shoulder. He took my right hand, palm up and drew a red X with his finger. He had me kneel down in a child's pose (I knew that from yoga). He then took two fingers and placed them at the bottom of my skull and traced his fingers down my spine.

Then I woke up.

It was no dream. I was at my own blessing ceremony. I do know that man, he's my Teacher. He's my Chief.

Months later (after this realization) I was at my first ever acupuncture appointment. While I was lying on the table, the Dr. of Oriental Medicine, with whom this was my 1st meeting, said to me, "Um, do you happen to know a really large imposing man dressed all in red?" I said simply, yet confidently, "Yes, I do. That's my Chief." She chuckled and said, "Well, just so you know, he showed up here before you did and wants to know what the heck I'm planning on doing to you today because there's nothing wrong with you." Chief continues to show up to all my appointments before me, always watching.

~Arnette

**Acknowledge that you are not alone
and forever will you feel their embrace.**

~Abraham

EVERYONE HAS THEM: CHAKRAS

The body has seven (7) major energy centers, each referred to as a *chakra*. You may have been introduced to them while participating in Yoga. The chakras must be kept unblocked to live a life of allowing. If a chakra is blocked, your own energy cannot flow freely. If a chakra is blocked, Source Energy cannot flow freely. Blockages can cause physical or emotional distress. The goal of the healer is to help the recipient have balanced chakras.

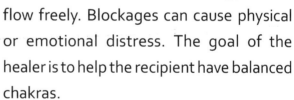

7th (white) The Crown Chakra represents our ability to be fully connected spiritually

6th (purple) the Third Eye Chakra represents our ability to focus and see the big picture

5th (blue): The Throat Chakra represents our ability to communicate

4th (green): The Heart Chakra represents our ability to give and receive love

3rd (yellow): The Solar Plexus Chakra represents our ability to be confident and in control

2nd (orange): The Sacral Chakra represents our ability to accept others and new experiences

1st (red): The Root Chakra represents our foundation and being grounded

How do I know if a Chakra is blocked? Ask.

The most practical way to ask if a chakra is open or closed is by using a **pendulum**. A pendulum is simply a tool used to receive a yes or no answer to a question. The pendulum is able to swing based on the energy that surrounds it. The direction of the pendulum's swing dictates an answer. The pendulum is a natural extension of an individual skilled in the art of healing, similar to how a stethoscope is a tool for a physician.

Pendulums come in a variety of shapes and sizes, from very simple to very ornate. They can be representative of the healer that uses it. Find a pendulum you find pleasing. Hold it as instructed and say "Show me

movement." If you have been practicing meditation and yoga, your vibration may be high enough to receive a swing. That is your pendulum! If there is no movement, try another. Do not be disappointed if you receive no movement. Simply select the pendulum that speaks to you the most.

A pendulum must be *cleared* and *programmed* before it will respond correctly. Always begin with a prayer of protection:

Holy Creator (God, Allah, etc.)
Please surround me in white light and protect me
As I ask my Spirit Guides and Angels
to help me in using this tool
As a way to communicate with the
energies around me and for me
Always on behalf of my highest self, never ego

Arnette's pendulum swings clockwise for a "yes." It swings north and south (vs. east/west) for a "no." Pendulums do respond differently, however, it can be programmed to respond in a way that is more comfortable to you. Ask the store personnel to assist you; they are most helpful. Some individuals are more vibrationally inclined and can move just about any pendulum they pick up. Do not despair if it takes awhile, practice makes perfect. Most likely, a pendulum will swing immediately for the Indigo the very first time! Asking questions of a pendulum cannot tell the future, it is a tool to assist "right here, right now," which is all that matters anyway.

Using the pendulum to determine if a chakra is blocked is an easy exercise. Simply hold the pendulum in front of the root chakra, receive confirmation of yes. Move to the sacral chakra and so on through the crown chakra. If the pendulum swings a no, direct it to "open" and show yes...and it will! Why is this important? It is important for you to be balanced. A negative emotion can block a chakra. You want to have free flowing energy at all times. If you are struggling with heartburn, bring balance to your solar plexus chakra. If you've ended a romantic relationship, bring balance to your heart chakra. If you are invited to an event where you have to socialize, bring balance to your throat chakra. The goal of life is to not struggle, but to allow everything in your life to easily *flow.*

**With balanced chakras the benefits are
endless, the lesson is timeless.**

~Abraham

A BEACON OF LIGHT

Spirits are souls that did not cross over, they did not follow the light when it was their time, possibly because they were afraid, or they had unfinished business, or just delayed a moment too long and lost their opportunity. They will wander, looking for the light. They are attracted to Indigo Souls because their essence is "light." They mean no harm. These spirits want you to be aware of them because you have the ability to help them cross over.

Negative Entities are a type of spirit intrusion. It may crave the energy of a physical body so it will attach to a person. This can actually disrupt that person's behavior. Negative Entities are especially drawn to the essence/light of an Indigo Soul. The more you evolve in your own personal growth the more open you are to this type of attachment as well.

Everyone has an energy field that other people step in or through. The more people near, or around you, increases the risk of picking up a negative intrusion. Think of the areas where you are exposed to crowds: the airport, a movie theater, a concert. If you are emotionally low or if you are weak due to illness, the more susceptible the body becomes.

How do I know if Negative Entities are present? Ask.

Do not be afraid. Prior to any attempt at communication, always protect yourself. The action of "asking" is raising your vibration, which in turn attracts both good and bad energies. Therefore, hold your pendulum and begin with a prayer. This is a simple and straightforward example:

Holy Creator (God, Allah, etc.)
Please surround me with your white light and protect me
As I ask for guidance from my Spirit
Guides and Angels at this time
Always on behalf of my highest self, never ego

{your pendulum should begin to swing yes as
they come in, and then ask it to stop}

Do I have any negative entities on me at this time (yes/no)

If no:

say thank you and ask for continued
love and protection for yourself

If yes:

find out how many using yes/no questions to get a count

Option1: Firmly tell the negative entity to leave. If you are inside, open a window or door. It was not invited here. It cannot stay. Continue to force the issue until your pendulum confirms it is gone. Unfortunately, it will just find another energy source on which to attach.

Option 2: Ask the Arch Angels for assistance. Call in Archangel Michael or Raphael to assist in removing this negative entity. Ask to surround it in white light. Explain that this entity was not invited here and it cannot stay. Request that the Angels escort the entity from the premises. Use your pendulum to confirm it is gone. Always thank the Angels. Wave your arm up and down around your body to cut any chords of energy the entity may have left behind.

As your Indigo vibration continues to increase, both you and your home become even more of a beacon for uninvited guests. It will continue to be a constant battle to keep your space and your loved ones "clear." Be diligent in establishing a routine: pay attention to what is, but more importantly what is not, typical behavior for the people living in your home. If you validate a presence, clear it. It can be a challenge. If you feel depressed, "in a funk", or you catch yourself being short tempered for no reason, check yourself. Preferably, reach out to other Indigos in your circle or "village" and have them check on your behalf.

~Arnette & Abraham

WALTZ INTO YOUR DHARMA

The ultimate goal for you, our Indigo Scout, is to find peace with your Karmic past. Realize that everything you have experienced, in this lifetime, is for that of a greater good.

Embrace and be one with the natural laws of the universe. Remember your lessons and the choices you make. Continue to choose YOU. You may be continuously tested with the same lessons over and over again. Continue to choose YOU. Think cause and effect. Do not engage if the situation is repetitive behavior. Make a conscious choice to do things differently. Step to the side momentarily, if you must. Yet always continue to move forward. Trust yourself to remember what it was like before others told you what to think, what to feel, what to be.

One definition of Dharma is from Hinduism: the principle of cosmic order: virtue, righteousness, and duty, especially social and caste duty in accord with the cosmic order. [11]

---

[11] http://oxforddictionaries.com/us/definition/american_english/dharma

You are stronger. You are wiser. You have evolved to rise above the limitations put upon you and reach for the stars. You know these stars. You come from these stars. Gaze upon them in wonder and realize that your singular importance is like that of a star. Together with your Indigo Soul brothers and sisters, you are delivering God's will to planet Earth.

Individually you heal.
Collectively you bring balance.

~Abraham & Arnette

AM I READY NOW?

DISCOVER YOUR AFFINITY

We have accurately communicated that the purpose of the Indigo Soul is to heal. However, the purpose of an Indigo Scout is to heal "now." Heal what? Why, everything, of course! Your Indigo Soul resonates with all energy: people, animals, and Earth. It is ingrained, in you, to be a human being with *feeling*. There are many other humans on Earth, right here right now, that have very different paths to which they must follow. Your path, dear Indigo, is to now simply honor yourself. Recognize you have boundaries. Do not be afraid to choose YOU.

~Abraham

Is my affinity for people?

Reflect on your life so far. Have you found what brings you the most joy? Are you the adult at a family gathering that would rather interact with the children? When you were growing up, were you the young one that had no friends your own age, but gravitated toward people that were older than you? Are you the person that would laugh and laugh at your grandparent's antics, even if it left your own parents bewildered? Do you have the courage to stand up to a bully on behalf of someone else? Do you feel sadness or anger over the choices others make that are an injustice? If yes, you have an affinity for people. You are meant to serve here.

SENIOR

Assisted Living
Hospice

ADOLECENT

Wellness
Illness
Injury/Illness
Hospice

ADULT

Wellness
Illness
Injury/Illness
Hospice

PEDIATRIC

Wellness
Illness
Injury/Illness
Hospice

Is my affinity for animals?

Reflect on your life so far. Have you found what brings you the most joy? Are you like the Indigo Scout Catherine (pg. 77) who loves horses? Or might it be another of God's creatures like dogs or cats? Maybe it is a fascination with sharks, dolphins, or whales? Could it be the amazing animals that live in the jungle or roam the plains? Do you find patience with the critters that should stay outside instead of finding their way into your home, like a rodent, lizard, or snake? You have an affinity for animals. Big or small, short or tall, it makes no difference. You are meant to serve here.

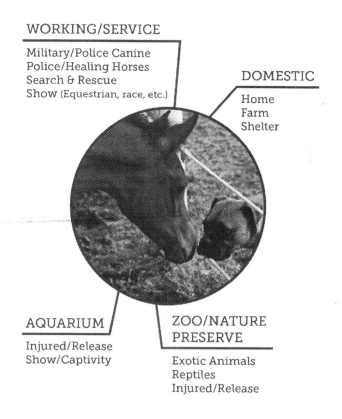

WORKING/SERVICE

Military/Police Canine
Police/Healing Horses
Search & Rescue
Show (Equestrian, race, etc.)

DOMESTIC

Home
Farm
Shelter

AQUARIUM

Injured/Release
Show/Captivity

ZOO/NATURE PRESERVE

Exotic Animals
Reptiles
Injured/Release

Is my affinity for the Earth (environment)?

Reflect on your life so far. Have you found what brings you the most joy? Do you spend as much time as possible out-of-doors? Does it matter if there is rain or shine? Do your senses flourish with the smells and colors of nature? Do you find peace and serenity laying in the shade of a tree, listening to the sounds all around you? Do you feel intense sadness or anger when learning about the destruction of forests by wild fires, or by the senseless contamination of water supplies through toxic spills? If you could have a conversation with Mother Nature do you already have a list of questions to ask? If yes, you have an affinity for the environment. You are meant to serve here.

AGRICULTURE

Farm/Crops
Orchard
Forest Restoration
Natural Resources

INDUSTRIAL
POLLUTION

Air
Toxic Spills

NATURAL
DISASTER

Fire
Tornado
Hurricane/Tsunami
Flooding
Earthquake

WATER

Salt Water
Fresh Water
Drinking Water

ACTIVATE THE HEALER IN YOU

Mikao Usui
Founder of Reiki

If the purpose of the Indigo Soul is to heal through Source Energy, how do you do that? The preferred modality is through USUI Reiki. Founded by Mikao Usui, USUI Reiki is the universal art of natural healing that positively affects the whole person including the body, emotions, mind, and spirit. The word Reiki means "universal life force energy."

God intended for Reiki to be handed down generation through generation with love, care, guidance and <u>practice</u>. It should have been fully embraced knowing its origin. This, and other ancient art forms, is God's natural way to extend and maintain harmony *energetically* for all God's creatures. It has been blatantly ignored. Its validity has been questioned out of fear or misunderstanding. In western culture, why was the name Reiki modified to bio-energetic healing? To make it more "accessible"? Was it modified because it cannot be seen by the naked eye?

Encouraging people to be proactive vs. reactive with their own health is fundamental. Being an advocate for the message is just as important as providing the Reiki.

~Arnette

The evolution of the modern world has come with detrimental effects. God sent the Indigo to administer "super charged" Reiki.

~Daniel Viotto

There are many skilled Reiki Masters who have taught this ancient art form effectively and will continue to do so. However, <u>how</u> an Indigo Soul is instructed is more important than the Reiki itself. You see, an Indigo Soul has administered Reiki many, many times before. They are, already, Masters. In this lifetime, the teacher of an Indigo Soul must be <u>more than</u> a Reiki Master. A teacher must be prepared to help the Indigo Soul *unlock the memories to remember the purpose.*

**Indigo Souls will surpass their teachers;
it can be no other way.**

~Abraham

Guidelines for Indigos seeking instruction

❖ Search for instruction that provides an overall solid foundation as to how you can reach your full Indigo potential.

❖ Align yourself with an Indigo Certified Reiki Master.

❖ Receive your instruction one-on-one. There is a lot of "undoing" that must be addressed.

❖ Receive instruction out of doors, in nature, with nature.

❖ Be re-introduced to your Angels and Spirit Guides. This is important for you to be the most effective healer you can be.

❖ Practice giving and receiving Reiki with other Indigos (Indigo on Indigo). As Indigo knows Indigo, working through your Karmic lessons will be cathartic.

❖ Follow your intuition...you know better than most.

❖ Step into your role as a Certified Indigo Healer™.

Remember, God sent you to heal. Begin to heal that which is broken. Heal the planet, the animals, but most of all, each other. You are here to bring balance back to Earth. Indigos are meant to blend their energy, alongside Source (God's) energy, to make it safe for the next wave of souls that are coming.

~Arnette & Abraham

GOINDIGO™ ... HONORING THE PURPOSE OF INDIGO ENERGY

Abraham assembled GoIndigo™ with a highly qualified team of Indigo Aware resources. Together we have the strategic vision to bring forth healing through Indigo and Source Energy. The GoIndigo™ Center focuses on the Indigo Soul. Not normally found in traditional higher-education and trade schools, we have developed a methodology which support learning *Indigo Style*. We focus specifically on content Abraham has deemed necessary to prepare an Indigo Soul in leading a life of purposeful healing.

As the Indigo Soul reaches their vibrational peak, additional gifts come forth. Key partnerships with specialized Earth Angels/Light Workers are more necessary than ever. There is a depth of knowledge, years of accumulated experiences, spread worldwide. We must transition this legacy knowledge to the Indigos. Are you an Earth Angel that has a gift that must be passed on?

**Indigo Energy must bring balance to Earth
to make Earth safe for the next wave of Souls to arrive.**

~Arnette & Abraham

ENERGIES WERE
ALIGNING ALL ALONG

In early 2004, I moved from Michigan to Texas. In late 2004, a couple from California relocated to Texas as well, Dan and Karen Viotto. Our paths crossed through mutual friends. It seems strange that we would even connect socially. I was a single mom with elementary school aged children. They have no children. It was slow, yet steady, spending more and more time together. I always appreciated Dan and his corporate background. We both had the same upbringing with families that expected us to be *achievers*. We would easily share our professional experiences (and bore Karen to tears). It never crossed either of our minds to be anything other than what we were...white collar workers climbing the corporate ladder. Karen and I have similar backgrounds in education. With flexible schedules it was relatively easy to meet for lunch. We'd talk about the education system, how and why my kids were struggling. Yet it was the three of us together that was an interesting dynamic. We shared "other worldly" concepts, books, and experiences. It began to make sense. We had to have known each other before (previous lifetimes). There had to be a reason we were together now.

~Arnette

FOUNDING GOINDIGO™

Abraham has a vision. Bring a core group of people together with very specific learned behaviors. Awaken the desire to reclaim their "knowing" all at the same time. Introduce select pieces of information in and around "Indigo." They will take care of the rest. "They" is Karen Viotto, Dan Viotto, and me! We are a bridge between the traditional non-Indigo and **Indigo** populations. Karen is blessed with the ability to unlock the healing abilities of an Indigo Soul, teaching the way they learn. She ignites awareness "in them" way beyond anything we, ourselves, had ever experienced. Dan radiates with an amazingly high vibration allowing him to understand, and easily convey, that which cannot be seen. He brings to life a corporate vision that is God's intent for the Indigo Soul. His messaging is transparent, with no hidden agenda. Me? I have the ability to hear the words of Abraham and write their message. In addition, I am able to introduce an Indigo to their Angels and Spirit Guides (all newly acquired skills, believe me!). We have the combined skill set to build a centralized infrastructure and solution for the purpose of Indigo. We called it GoIndigo™.

The message extends way beyond a parent or guardian navigating society on behalf of the Indigo Soul in their care. The message extends to the Indigo Scouts that are here on Earth and can feel the "shift" in their entire being. They are being called home.

~Arnette

BE INSPIRED
STORIES of GoIndigo™ INDIGO SCOUTS
stepping into purpose
(names have been changed to respect privacy)

Russell A.

During my weekly lunches with Karen Viotto she would sometimes mention a co-worker commenting on his intuitiveness and gentleness. He gave us permission to ask if he was indeed an Indigo. Although I was not with him when he received the news, apparently the answer was received with both relief and anticipation. Karen soon spent a day unlocking Russell's Reiki and provided his attunement. Afterwards I met up with them for lunch. This was my first meeting with the Indigo Scout named Russell.

Conversation flowed easily as he gave us a brief history of his upbringing. We finally arrived at my house and waited for Elizabeth (another Indigo Scout) to arrive. One thing I learned from Abraham, is that an Indigo Soul should not "practice their craft" on either Karen or me. Their energy is powerful. She and

I have worked too long to reach the vibration we are at while still keeping ourselves in balance.

"Pair Indigo with Indigo for any hands-on practice, Arnette. This is very important." Abraham would tell me. Learning later that their energy "seeks a like" energy.

When Elizabeth arrived, she had a friend with her. Elizabeth was willing to forfeit her Reiki session so that her friend could receive; not knowing that we needed Indigo on Indigo. I didn't know this person. Though this girl seemed in control of her emotions, Elizabeth followed her intuition and brought her anyway knowing her friend needed assistance. With a brief explanation, she gave us permission and we were able to confirm she was Indigo as well. The universe provided Russell with two Indigos for Reiki practice this day!

Karen demonstrated the correct hand positions with Russell following close behind. Eventually Karen silently stepped aside and allowed Russell to continue. After the session was completed, and not knowing what to expect, the friend was able to articulate what she had "felt." With Karen, it was gentle waves of energy that felt warm and comforting. However, with Russell, the energy actually buzzed and radiated, sending pulses through her body. This girl did not know that the purpose of an Indigo Soul is to heal. She did not know that an Indigo Soul can transmit a higher vibrational energy and more of it, than a non-Indigo. Karen and I smiled at each other knowing what we were witnessing. To an Indigo, receiving traditional

Reiki healing probably feels like a single bee. Whereas, Indigo-on-Indigo Reiki is like a *swarm* of bees (just not with the sting)!

When Elizabeth and her friend left, Russell was able to communicate his own thoughts and feelings. How natural if felt to be doing what he was doing. He was very emotional in explaining how hard it was growing up. Thinking he was no different than the other children in school, but made to feel anything but the same. Being placed in "special education" classes and separated from the rest of the class shattered his already sensitive nature. He was "accepted" he says, because he was a really good athlete. He distinctly remembers the day a coach pulled him aside and said, "You really need to get your act together or you'll never amount to anything." He has struggled to find his place...always.

When we were finishing out the day, Russell said how disappointed he was that he himself had not received Reiki. Elizabeth was not yet qualified to give. Karen and I agreed to provide Reiki to Russell. We figured two Reiki Masters should be able to flow enough Source energy for this loving Indigo Soul to receive. Karen positioned herself at Russell's feet, and I stood at his head. We prayed, "Dear holy creator, please surround us in white light as we ask for guidance from Russell's Spirit Guides and Angels at this time; always on behalf of his highest self, never for ego."

I was immediately overwhelmed with, not only a flood of energy, but also with a flood of tears. I couldn't contain them as I lifted my face and my teary eyes connected with Karen's. She could see the shock register on my face, and I struggled with what I was hearing. "Your Angels are here, Russell, there are 4," I said. I also said in my mind, "only 4?" That number seemed low. The response, "We are very powerful Angels." I said the first name out loud. It was a very unique name, as was the second. I knew I would not remember and I quickly grabbed paper to write down the names of the third and forth Angels. Still my tears flowed. I was self conscious and embarrassed that I could not contain my emotions, "seriously Arnette", I said to myself, "pull yourself together." I could see Karen had silent tears rolling down her face. We moved in perfect unison around Russell; pulling out energy and replacing it with new. The words continued to come, "You are very blessed to be working with this Indigo Soul, take great care, for he is very powerful," his Angel said to me.

After I mopped my face and blew my nose, and nervously giggled at the mess I'd become, Russell slowly came back to awareness. He said he was going in and out of consciousness the entire time he was on the table. When he heard the first Angel name, he thought to himself, "I know that name." He also indicated that as he lay there, the entire time it felt like it was raining on his skin. We laughed and said it was probably all of our tears. His own emotions were bubbling so closely under the surface as he uttered the most profound statement, "I feel like I'm home." At that point, Karen and I both understood the magnitude of what Abraham has been positioning us to do. I am not a Navigator for just my own children that are Indigo Souls; I am a Navigator for all Indigo Souls. Karen is their Indigo Master Teacher.

I relayed this event to my dear friend Holly Stamps. Holly plays a critical role for me in that I often struggle with doubt and my own worthiness as I grow into this Navigator role. She is the mother of two Indigo Souls both in their early 20's. In addition, she was a youth minister for many, many years. She brings a unique perspective for me and I welcome her insight. After I finished retelling the story about Russell, she says "Arnette, have you ever heard the term *tears from heaven?*" Of course I have not. I have no formal faith foundation at all. She continues "my understanding is that *tears from heaven* are a type of blessing. I don't think those were your tears. I want you to ask Abraham for clarification on the event that occurred." "Interesting", I thought. I very rarely ask Abraham questions because I don't know what to ask. Abraham normally just guides me along giving me the information to be conveyed. I was excited that for once, I actually had a really good question. I asked. And this was my answer:

> *These tears are a blessing from Heaven*
> *Allow them to fall like rain*
> *See the reflection of your Soul in her eyes*
> *Tears of Joy, for You, our Indigo*
> *That you have found your way home*
> *~Abraham~*

When my eyes connected with Karen's, even through all our tears, I know she could see my soul and I could see hers. I will never doubt my purpose again.

Elizabeth H.

I live in Austin, Texas. Self proclaimed as the *live music capital of the world*. Elizabeth and I met four years ago at a venue where live music was playing. We both dated musicians at the time so had this one, precarious thing, in common. We ran into each other occasionally and it was always fun. She's bright and funny. I found her very endearing. I'm quite a few years older than Elizabeth and always felt like a Mom. If I was lucky, possibly, I'd feel like just an older sister. Occasionally we would get together, just the two of us. Unfortunately, it was usually because she was in crisis and needed someone to talk to.

I knew from our previous discussions that her upbringing was anything but ideal: parents that loved her but didn't understand her. Elizabeth was very self destructive from a very early age. She admits that when it came to school, her methodology for success was anything but normal, basically having to rewrite entire books and notes into a unique format for consumption, understanding, and recall. She was stubborn and had a strong conviction that she <u>would</u> make it through school. Even though she had graduated from the University of Texas, finding that feeling of satisfaction and self worth eluded her. Elizabeth left Austin for a three month sabbatical in Costa Rica. She desperately needed to reconnect with the essence of what she was. She'd gotten lost somewhere along the way.

Upon her return, we agreed to meet for dinner just to catch up. I had never talked to her about any of my writing or work with Indigos. I've found that it's not something to just blurt out; it deserves respect and the right audience. I didn't know what to expect from this dinner, but I was very excited to see her. She looked healthy, vibrant and very "present." We got through the idle chit-chat and she started to dive into the details of her trip. Returning to the yoga immersion program did not provide her with what she was looking for. She also got very ill. An Austin transplant now living in Costa Rica nursed her back to health. Using pure essential oils and her ability to work with Angels, this woman shared that fact that she was Indigo. She confirmed that Elizabeth was Indigo as well. "Arnette," Elizabeth said, "do you know anything about Indigo?"

The energy between us was electric and the information just started to flow. Her biggest fear coming back from Costa Rica was not finding her village of support. I assured her she was an Indigo Scout with a very important role at the GoIndigo™ Center. We agreed that in exchange for her Reiki training she would teach Kundalini Yoga, which Abraham said was important for both Karen and me to embrace. We shopped together for Elizabeth's first pendulum, such an important tool for any holistic healer. She walked away with four. After our first yoga session together, she asked if I could introduce her to her Angels. At that point in time, I said I didn't know. I'd only met my own. I had no idea if I could do it for others. She sat outside with paper and pencil and I listened. The names came fast! But it was specifically the last Angel name I gave her when her eyes slowly raised, wide and in wonder, and connected with mine. "Every doll I played with when I was little I named them *Justine*." All along she was playing with an Angel.

Karen unlocked Elizabeth's Reiki with her attunement outside on a hot, hot day in Austin. She was wiped out and I was told by her Angels and Spirit Guides that she was unable to do her Reiki practical at this time. It would have to wait for another day. Disappointed, but understanding, she received Reiki from us instead. It was time for her blessing. Because we had previously met her Angels, I positioned myself at her feet, where Spirit Guides come to me. The one thing about a Reiki attunement is that is brings forth unfinished life lessons to the surface. The body will not only detox physically, but also emotionally. Our tears from heaven blessed her soul. Her own tears cleansed her soul. Karen and I embraced Elizabeth as she thanked us and called us "mama bears." Through her sniffles and with a muffled voice we could hear her faintly say, "I finally feel like I'm home." Karen and I just shook our heads and smiled at each other; we had brought another Indigo home.

Abraham specifically told me how important Kundalini Yoga is for the Indigo Souls. So of course God sent us Elizabeth, an Indigo Soul that instructs Kundalini Yoga! Elizabeth is at the beginning of her transformation to becoming the powerful healer God sent her here to be. She is fortunate to have a most powerful Spirit Guide Teacher, a shaman, whom is also a father from a past life! How lucky am I to have a front row seat to watch all the Indigo Souls that will flourish under Elizabeth's tutelage!

Natasha S.

I used to ride my bike across the street to this tiny little gym for strength training. One of the trainers there was a nice young transplant from England named Natasha. Months went by and we never really said more than hello and goodbye. But her energy was infectious, and her smile contagious. I don't even know how the conversation started, maybe it was about a book we had in common, but it must have been an "out of the ordinary" book that made me wonder "Is Natasha Indigo?" It's not my right to be nosey and just ask about someone. I need their permission.

I had written an essay about my son and his struggles with traditional education. I felt compelled to share it with Natasha. It opened the door for conversation and learning more about each other.

Natasha really struggled growing up, not only academically, but also socially. She never quite fit in. Some members of her own family didn't really support or nurture the sensitive side of her nature. It was insisted that she go to university for the opportunity to have a "good solid job". She did, obtaining a degree as a graphic artist. Although very artistic and talented, graphic design is a job, it's not her passion. She came to the United States, and left to her own devices, focused on personal fitness and working with people. She immersed herself in nutrition and yoga, yet continued to struggle in finding her place. I suggested she see my Dr. of Oriental Medicine, Cindy Nilson, and possibly see my Life-Path Mentor, Linda Drake.

By now my essay had morphed into a book: *The Indigo Soul: a child's journey to purpose* was my first collaboration with Abraham. I shared the manuscript. Our next meeting began with Natasha all flustered, "Enough already, I have to know right now, am I Indigo?" So we asked, and yes Natasha, you are indeed Indigo. The universe provided me with an Indigo that was also a graphic designer? Who better to design the cover of that book! Everything about and around GoIndigo™ is for you Natasha, an Indigo Soul.

Natasha had already gone for Reiki training and explained how she felt physically ill when she was there. I really wanted her to spend the time with Karen and receive the "Indigo Unlock" as we now started referring to it internally at GoIndigo™. Her events unfolded a little backwards since I was leaving soon on a holiday. Natasha ended up receiving her blessing from Abraham before working with Karen. On blessing day, Karen positioned herself at Natasha's feet and I stood at her head.

This time when the tears came, I wasn't embarrassed or self-conscious because I knew exactly what they meant. Her Angels came first, five of them, and introduced themselves. Again in perfect unison, Karen and I moved energy out and in. While standing at her feet, her Spirit Guides came forth. I will leave out personal tidbits of what they said, just know that the things I said out loud, I never could have known. Soon Karen and I heard the words we'd been waiting for. It's like music to our ears as Natasha said through tears of joy, "No, no, you don't understand, I feel like I'm home."

It is wonderful that Karen and I are able to "unlock" an Indigo. However, it definitely can force emotional blocks to the surface. Another Indigo knows how to truly identify and help with healing that pain. During a Reiki exchange between Natasha and Elizabeth, the intuitiveness with each other, for each other, was remarkable. Natasha's vibration is now soaring to new heights. As she steps into her role, the transformation of her spirit is apparent to us all. We are so lucky to have her on our team.

Catherine L.

Little did we know then, but the universe brought Catherine and me together over 10 years ago for a reason. Being mothers as well as strong women in the corporate world with more or less the same skill set, drive, and personality type, we clicked instantly. We always enjoyed spending time together, although limited, due to busy schedules and families. Even after I moved from Michigan to Texas, we stayed in touch, and I always stay at her home when I travel back for my annual visit.

Catherine is a very private person and doesn't share personal details with many. Although she had shared bits and pieces of her life with me over the years, I only knew her as strong, confident, and always in control.

As Indigo became such a focal point in my own personal development, I felt I could share with her everything I was learning. She was always attentive and interested in what I had to say. Through the years, Catherine had obtained a unique skill-set that could help me with the website development for GoIndigo.com. To lay a foundation, I sent her my manuscript for *The Indigo Soul: a child's journey to purpose.* I had always suspected her daughter, at age seven, was an Indigo Soul. After reading it, she gave me permission to ask. The answer was a definite yes. Her daughter had a strong affinity for both animals and people. I was confident Catherine was a Navigator just like me.

In the summer of 2013, I scheduled three days to spend at her home where we could focus our time on the website. From the moment we saw each other it was non-stop talking about everything that was going on with establishing GoIndigo™. As the evening wore on, I could not ignore the voice in my head telling me that SHE was an Indigo Scout. What I didn't know was she was wondering the same thing. My logical brain was having trouble with this concept. The Indigo Scouts that I have worked with so far were very similar in nature. In my mind, Catherine was nothing like them. She was everything like me. I couldn't ignore the hairs all over my body standing on end.

I asked her point blank "After everything we've talked about and everything you've researched on your own about Ava, did it cross your mind that you might be Indigo as well?" She looked me straight in the eye and said "yes." With her permission, I called in her Angels and Spirit Guides. We confirmed that yes she was, indeed, Indigo. Due to her age, she falls into the Indigo Scout category, meaning she was left to her own devices in finding her path to healing. She had no one to help navigate her as a child. She does, however, have me to navigate her now. The tables had turned and I sat, attentive and interested and said, "Tell me." And she did.

Catherine was given up for adoption immediately after she was born, never bonding with her birth mother. To this day, she still doesn't understand why she was placed with an older couple who already had five, much older, biological children of their own. Her childhood was a struggle to say the least. There was a lot of violence and substance abuse around her with her adoptive siblings. The family didn't have much money, structure, or support. She knew, without a doubt, she would do anything to get out. Catherine has always preferred the company of animals over people, being obsessed with horses for as long as she can remember. Oddly her family never had horses, nor contact with anyone who did. In fact, they lived in town. Her parents couldn't understand where this obsession came from, thinking it was just a phase. At age seven, after two years of begging them for a horse, they realized it wasn't a phase. They found a barn that would let her come out and do odd jobs, which she did just so she could be around the horses. That was the beginning of a lifetime with horses. From then on, Catherine worked any job she could to pay for the one thing that brought joy. This was her escape. Horses don't judge. Horses don't hurt. Horses only accept. Though difficult, she was able to maintain good grades knowing it would be her ticket out. When she left for college, she never looked back.

Years later, Catherine set out to locate her birth mother. Her search revealed that this woman lived in Michigan. She always had horses. Gave birth and raised two other daughters after having Catherine. Yet, she showed no desire to have any kind of relationship with her. Through years of struggle, Catherine became adept at turning off her emotions to cope. This hurt. This second rejection only fueled her drive. Horses, not people, continued to heal her soul.

As I mentioned before, I viewed Catherine as strong, confident, and always in control as most do who meet her. I was genuinely surprised as she confides in me saying that this bravado she has is all an illusion. She describes herself as a 'basket case' and has always struggled with insecurity and low self esteem. She shields herself with this wall of confidence that really isn't there. She tells me she's gotten this far driven by the fear of failure ("Failure is not an option"). I prefer to say on God's grace.

Catherine's corporate day job pays for this love of horses. After years of boarding at other stables, she decided that she could run a barn better than most. She was able to secure the loans necessary and opened an equestrian center. Boarding other people's horses helps fund her love. However, her ultimate goal is to rehabilitate, retrain, and re-home off-the-track thoroughbred (OTTB) race horses. After rescuing two OTTB's, she quickly began to realize the cost of this dream. After years of unrelenting veterinarian and specialist bills, the physical and emotional trauma these horses experience in their young lives still existed. "I want to fix them myself. I don't understand why I can't fix them, clearly traditional medicine is not working," she said. My response, "You can, and you will." Totally spur of the moment, Catherine had a crash course on chakras and the use of a pendulum. I introduced her to her team of Angels and Spirit Guides. As with all Indigo Scouts, she will need to release blame and shame to move her through her Karmic veil toward her Dharma. She scheduled a visit to Austin to spend time with Karen and me and to fill in the gaps of her "knowing."

Today, with 30 plus years in horse behavior modification, training, and conditioning, along with her Indigo Reiki, Catherine is well on her way to fulfilling her purpose as a

Certified Indigo Healer™ for God's majestic creature, the horse.

My lesson: Do not assume who may, or may not, be an Indigo Soul. God has wrapped them up in a variety of packages, and it is my purpose to make sure they are found and unwrapped.

Camille B.

Camille and I were introduced through mutual friends many years ago. We'd run into each other at the same places so eventually just ended up going to those places together. I was always drawn to her bubbly personality and carefree spirit, but also to the most crystal blue eyes I had ever seen in a human face. Over the years, bits and pieces were shared with me. Growing up with the challenges she had, a person could easily play the victim card, but she never did. She is resilient. She is a survivor.

When her father left when she was two, Camille was primarily raised by her grandparents. Though her mother was involved in her upbringing, it was always in a controlled environment, for Camille's own safety. Unfortunately, her mother battled with bouts of severe depression, eventually passing away when Camille was 16. It is common for a young woman to deal with grief in a self-destructive way, and she did. After losing her grandfather, she lived with, and cared for, her ailing grandmother. Until she, too, passed away. This is when we met.

As a young child, Camille remembers being able to "see" what most people could not. But, any discussion around her natural gift was completely dismissed as being fanciful or crazy. She learned to keep her eyes and ears open, and her mouth shut. Though never formally diagnosed with any medical condition such as ADD, ADHD, or dyslexia, she struggled with traditional education methods. Determined to attend college, I remember her telling me the story of driving unexpectedly to Mississippi University for Women insisting on being admitted. Everything on paper said she wasn't a good candidate. She graduated with a degree in Early Childhood Development "by the Grace of God." It was easy for me to share the academic challenges my own children faced. She would share with me her own stories that were so similar. And now, as a teacher, she is the "pied piper" to the kids that just don't seem to "fit." When the term *Indigo* first came to my attention, it was Camille who kept coming to my mind. I called her one day and said, "I think you are Indigo."

Camille is my barometer. She is my own personal cheering section. She wishes for the mom that could never support her the way I am able to with my kids. She wants to enlighten the parents of all the kids she comes in contact with as a teacher. More so, wanting to finally feel at peace with an "energetic pull" she could never quite grasp. We unlocked her Reiki.

We are sitting in the shade of an enormous oak tree on the banks of Barton Springs. A gentle breeze consistently blows all around. How nice to have a breeze since it's August in Austin. Karen, Camille, Camille's Navigator Emily, and I are ready for the long day ahead. Karen dreamed about Camille the night before. Emily dreamed about me. Our individual energies were aligning. *Instruction. Learning. Collaboration. Allowing.* All words to describe how we build a strong foundation.

We talk about how sometimes it's difficult to be your true authentic self around your own blood family. How fortunate are we to be constructing a "family of choice". How do four strangers from Michigan, Louisiana, and California find themselves in this position, right here, right now? Divine Guidance.

After lunch and Reiki attunements, it is time for Camille to be introduced to her Angels and Spirit Guides. I position myself at her head, Karen at her feet. Emily settles in to be a scribe for what is said. "You have seven Angels, Camille," I say, as my tears begin to flow. Her first five are lovely, supportive and kind. Her sixth Angel is more talkative with many words of encouragement. But, it is her last Angel that steps forward who is strong, powerful, commanding. He shimmers in sparkles of silver and light. I'm watching from behind him, through him, as he says, "You stood up in your crib and looked right at me Camille. Tell me you saw me. Tell me you remember." I can see her as he sees her: this little snippet of a girl, hanging on to the edge of her crib looking him straight in the eye. And I hear the voice of a little girl, from the body of the woman lying beneath my hands that whispers "I can see you."

Her Spirit Guides were eager to come forward. An animal totem, a Silverback Gorilla, was clearly evident. This was the first of many animal totems I am able to introduce to Indigos! However, the most empowering message from this blessing is in regards to the purpose of MODELING. Growing up Indigo is hard. It was hard for Camille and it's hard for the Indigos that are finding their way to her. But she lived, and continues to live, her life as an optimist. She chooses to embrace this lifetime with joy and eagerness for her purpose. She is the steady soul that will slowly bring awareness, sometimes with resistance to change, one Indigo at a time.

Emily N.

Camille introduced Emily and me years ago. "The closest thing to an Indigo without being Indigo," is how her Angels described her to me. A "pure navigator" by Abraham's definition. Unknowingly, at the time, Emily was stepping into her role of Navigator for Camille. They taught in the same school and were even roommates for a period of time. Emily is a bi-lingual speech pathologist. She works with a wide variety of children with various stages of development. In addition to this professional role, she also became yoga certified in her "spare time". What I find most interesting about Emily, is that she truly "walks the walk". Her body is her temple. She eats, breaths, and sleeps organic. She is a minimalist who will travel the world with only a backpack. She is a seeker of her own truth, wanting to learn what she can, when she can, from whomever she can. I have always admired her.

Most children model their parents. It's normal, it's expected. However, an Indigo Soul is not like the majority of the population on this planet. In the United States, if they are raised "the traditional way" with our current education system, competitive sports, eating mass produced foods, etc.; it is detrimental to their well being and natural vibration. More so, they will have a difficult time finding their way to purpose, as the life of a healer. I am also a Navigator, the parent or guardian of an Indigo Soul. Unlike Emily, I didn't know my son was Indigo until he was already 15 years old. I raised him as I was raised, in a traditional household doing traditional things, unaware of my own, let alone his, *knowing.*

My Indigo son is almost 20. Her Indigo son is not yet one. In order to reach his purpose, my son has to work through Western cultural challenges that were placed upon. Her son will have none.

I still would have been behind the 8-ball so to speak, even if I had known. I didn't eat properly, nor did I practice yoga, and I most certainly didn't know about meditation. Instead of nurturing his "knowing", I was subjecting him to overstimulation at an amusement park. Instead of hiking in the woods and swimming in the lake, I was screaming at him from the sidelines at some random sporting event. And for everything I didn't support, he now has to correct it within himself. It seems unfair, doesn't it? He has to unfix something that could have been prevented. If only I had known.

Emily does know. Her son will model her behavior as he grows. She is already eating clean, so her breast milk isn't passing on metals and toxins. She doesn't open a jar of baby food. Instead she cuts open an avocado and smooshes it herself. She continues to practice yoga and he is right there with her. She is protecting his energy by shielding it with her own. The list goes on and on.

It is time for the world to know. Please reach for *The Indigo Soul: a child's journey to purpose* if you know an adult who is raising an Indigo Soul. Our Indigo's deserve better.

Growing up Indigo I'm sure you have many ideas of what you wish had been different. Your parents did the best they could. Let us educate the parents of today, as to how to raise the Indigo for tomorrow. Follow Emily's lead. Lead by example.

WHAT NEXT?

When closing this book my wish is that these written words have resonated with you on a level so deep that you feel empowered and hopeful. Being raised non-Indigo, everything in this society, such as schools, jobs and lifestyles are geared toward me and people like me. I had never been proactive with my health, always reactive, until, I was made aware of Indigo Energy. Yet it is so important for everyone, parents and professionals alike, to understand that there IS a difference. Especially in understanding how "ultra sensitive" the Indigo Soul is. I don't mean that in a "don't be a big baby, you're so emotional" kind of way. Not at all! Sensitive: meaning "so *finitely* aware" of the energies around you, good and bad. Indigo have a heart rich in goodness and a bullshit detector so large it's unnerving.

We are all responsible for creating a safe environment for the Indigo Soul to flourish! It is more evident than ever that our current approach to education, the typical choices for extra-curricular activities, and what the mainstream job market has to offer, is not conducive to Indigo Souls, regardless of age. It is time to embrace Indigo Soul abilities with an open heart and an open mind. If you are non-Indigo, send thanks to the Heavens for sending them to us. If you are Indigo, thank you for coming.

Please visit www.goindigohealing.com for details on becoming a Certified Indigo Healer™ through The GoIndigo™ Center[12]. We look forward to greeting you at our open door.

~Arnette, Abraham and the GoIndigo™ Team

---

[12] **GoIndigo™** provides higher education via vocational & apprenticeship programs for Indigo and Autistic Indigo individuals in the area of bio-energetic healing. www.goindigohealing.com.